compact
music
guides
for
guitarists

BLUES GUITAR
CHORD REFERENCE

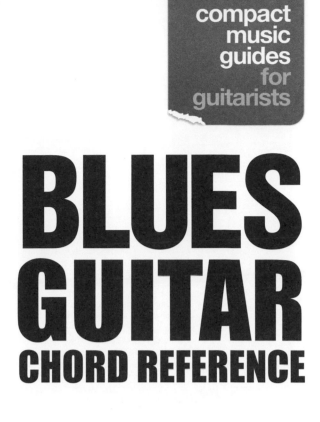

T0057734

HAL•LEONARD®

Cover design: Fresh Lemon
Interior design and layout: Len Vogler

Visit Hal Leonard Online at
www.halleonard.com

Order No. AM 91731
ISBN-13: 978-0-8256-3689-9

Printed in the UK

Contact us:
Hal Leonard
7777 West Bluemound Road Milwaukee, WI 53213
Email: info@halleonard.com

In Europe, contact:
Hal Leonard Europe Limited
42 Wigmore Street
Marylebone, London, W1U 2RY
Email: info@halleonardeurope.com

In Australia, contact:
Hal Leonard Australia Pty. Ltd.
4 Lentara Court
Cheltenham, Victoria, 3192 Australia
Email: info@halleonard.com.au

Contents

Introduction

This book is designed to teach you, in a clear way, the chords and progressions you will need to play songs in the blues form. Through the use of pictures and diagrams, the basic chords in each key become easily recognized and immediately useful.

The Compact Blues Guitar Chord Reference can be used as a step-by-step learning method, as a chord reference book, or as a practice guide to help strengthen your chord technique. Some blues songs have been added for both their interest and for practical application of the chords shown.

For best results, the beginner should proceed systematically, making sure he plays all the practice progressions and memorizes every chord, playing them until they can be fretted accurately and quickly. Once the chords in a particular key are learned thoroughly, they should be applied to these and other blues songs. There are many excellent blues songbooks on the market for further investigation of this fascinating field of music, and the student is encouraged to learn as many songs from books and records as he or she can.

The Compact Blues Guitar Chord Reference starts with the simplest first position chords, but progresses quickly to more complex positions, including bar chords and other movable patterns. This book will not only be useful in playing blues, but can increase your knowledge and technique for any kind of music, whether jazz, folk, rock, or pop.

How to hold the guitar

Chord Diagrams

The chord diagram is a picture, or a map, of the guitar fingerboard. Six vertical lines represent the six strings, and the shorter, horizontal lines represent the frets. Circles indicate the place at which the string is fretted, and the number within the circle indicates the finger of the left hand to be used. Each diagram is drawn as if the guitar were facing you, in a vertical position. Therefore, the sixth, or bass string, is on the left, and the first (the thinnest) is on the right.

An X next to a string indicates that the string is not strummed or picked with that particular chord. If there is no mark over the string, that string is played *open*, and is not fretted by the left hand.

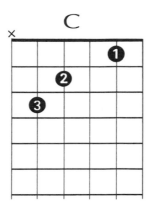

The Right Hand

Blues can be played either with a flatpick or with the fingers, depending on the kind of sound you want to get. A country blues guitarist will invariably play in a finger style, using the thumb on the bass notes while the fingers pick out the treble melody notes. A more modern player would tend to strum the chords with a flatpick in the manner of a jazz guitarist. This book is designed to teach you as many useful chords as possible, but I have also provided suggestions in tablature for both pick and finger style blues guitar patterns.

When playing the rhythms notated in this book, a slash mark / represents a one-beat strum across the strings of the guitar in a downward direction. A double slash mark // means that you strum an eighth note rhythm using a down-up stroke. These are included to give you an idea of the rhythmic possibilities in blues playing, and may be varied and improvised as much as you'd like.

Key of E

E

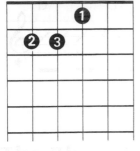

A7

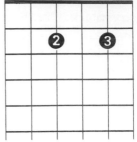

B7

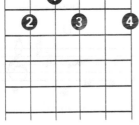

E7

Checkpoints

- Play each note with the tip of your finger so as not to touch the neighboring strings.

- Your fingers may become sore at first, but they will develop callouses and toughen up before long.

- Notice that in the E and B7 chords, your second finger **remains in the same position.** This will help when changing from one chord to the other.

12-Bar Blues Progression in E

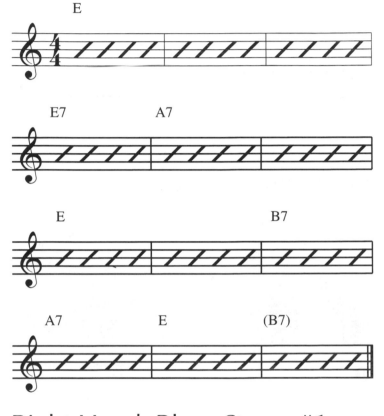

Right Hand: Blues Strum #1

Thumb picks a bass note. Index and middle fingers brush lightly down, then up, across the top three or four strings.

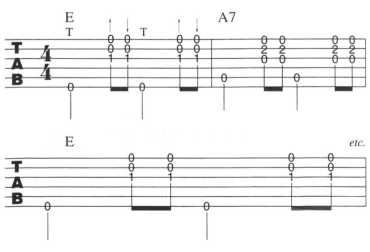

8-Bar Blues in E

Thumb picks the bass note.

Index and middle fingers brush lightly down, then up, across the top three or four strings.

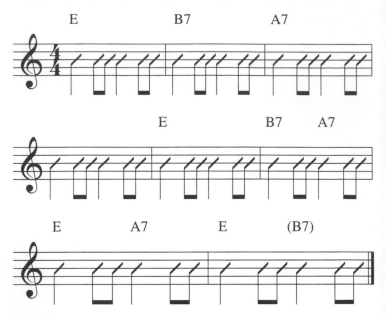

Key to the Highway

words & music by
Big Bill Broonzy and Charles Segar

I got the key to the

high - way, _____ Lord, I'm bound to

go. I'm gon- na leave here run - nin' _____

cause walk-in's much _ too slow. _____

Key of A

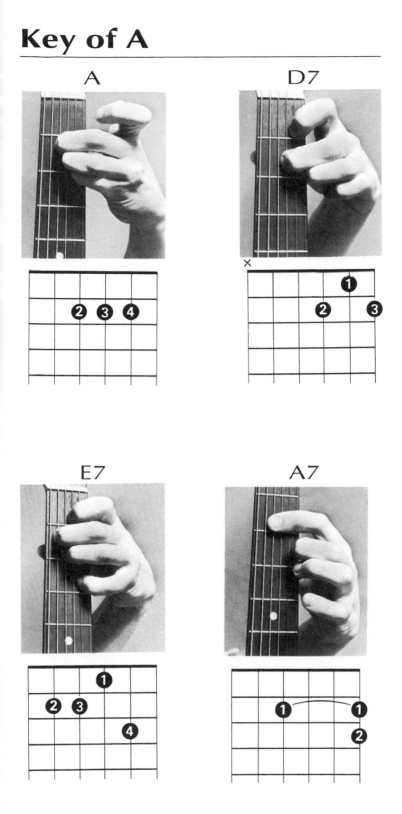

A

D7

E7

A7

Checkpoints

- Do not strum the 6th string while fretting D7.

- The E7 and A7 chords are different from those shown on page 6. They can be played inter-changeably, but each version of the chord has a distinctive sound. Play both versions to hear the difference.

- The A7 noted above utilizes a bar, in which your index finger plays four strings at the same fret. Keep your index finger straight and apply pressure with your thumb behind the neck so that you can fret all four strings evenly.

12-Bar Blues Progression in A

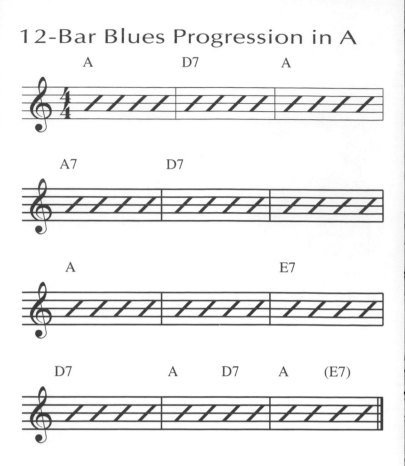

Right Hand: Blues Strum #2

Thumb picks a bass note.

Index and middle fingers brush lightly up-down-up across the top three or four strings. The rhythm has a bounce to it, accenting the bass and down-strokes.

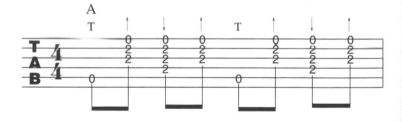

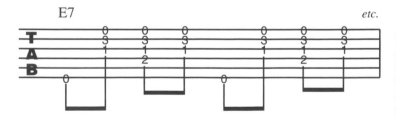

etc.

8-Bar Blues in A

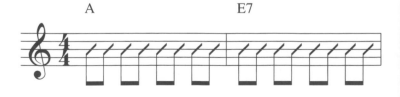

Matchbox Blues

Key of D

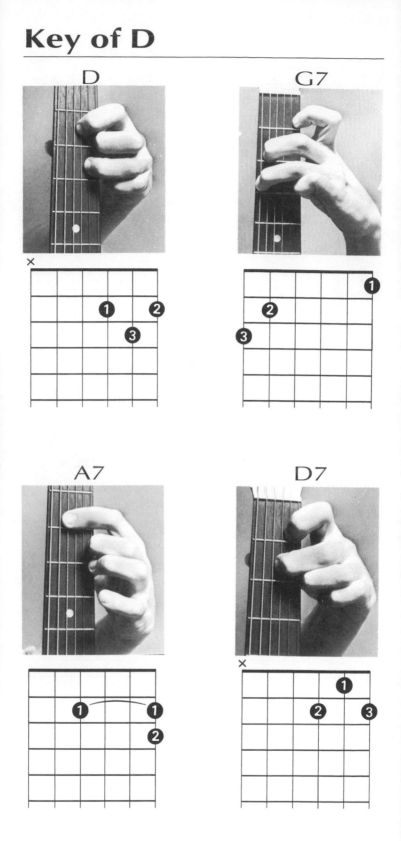

D   G7

A7   D7

Checkpoints

- Do not strum the 6th string with the D or D7 chords.

- Be sure you press the string close to the fret to prevent it from buzzing. This is especially important with G7

12

12-Bar Blues Progression in D

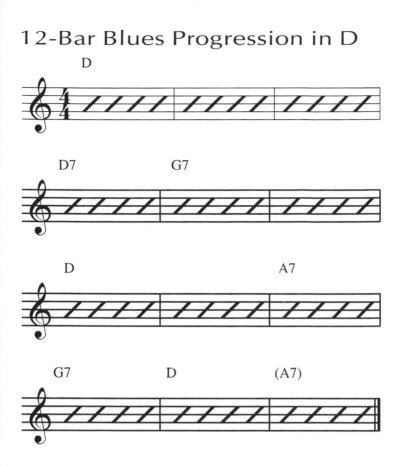

Right Hand: Blues Arpeggio #1

Thumb picks a bass note.

Index finger picks the 3rd string. Middle and ring fingers pick the 2nd and 1st strings together.

Index finger picks the 3rd string.

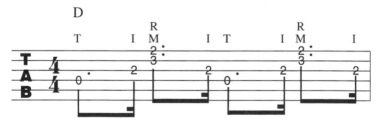

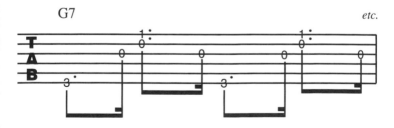

8-Bar Blues in D

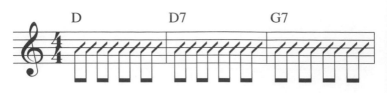

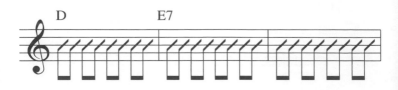

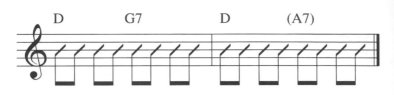

The Blues Ain't Nothin'

Well the blues ain't_ no - thin', no, the

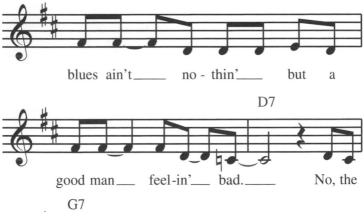

blues ain't____ no - thin'____ but a

good man__ feel-in'__ bad.____ No, the

blues ain't_ no-thin' but a good man feel-in'___

bad. It must have__ been __ those

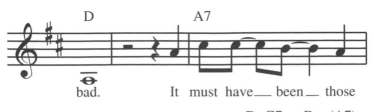

wear-y__ blues__ I had._____

Key of G

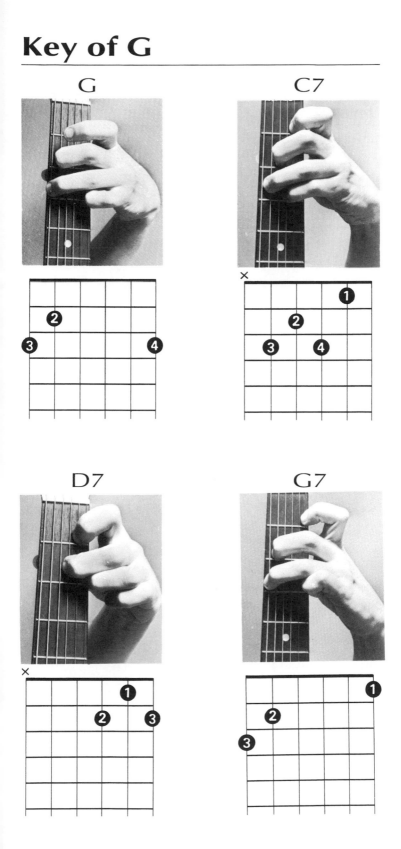

G C7

D7 G7

Checkpoints

- Do not play the 6th string with the C7 chord.

- If you are having trouble reaching all the notes in the G chord, try arching your wrist forward a little to bring your fingers closer to the fingerboard.

- Notice that in changing from G to G7, you don't have to move your second and third fingers.

12-Bar Blues Progression in G

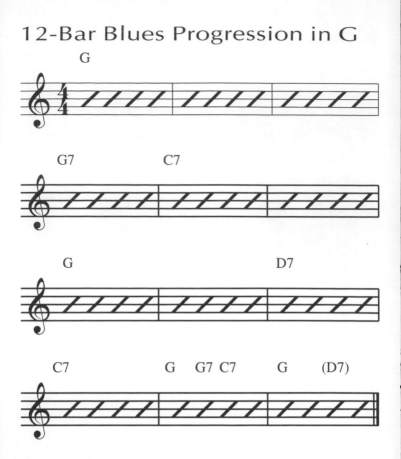

Right Hand: Combining Blues Strums #1 and #2

Thumb picks a bass note.

Index and middle finger brush down across the top strings.

Thumb picks a bass note.

Index and middle fingers brush up-down-up.

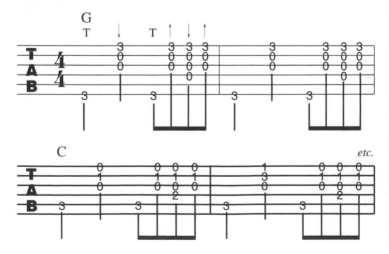

8-Bar Blues in G

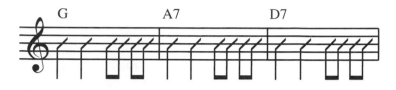

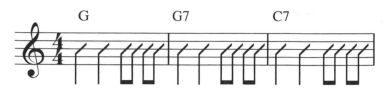

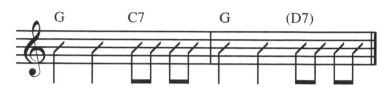

Step It Up and Go

Used to have a gal, she was lit-tle and low. She

used to love me but she don't no more. She had to

step it up and go,____ step it up and go.

She could-n't stay there, I de-

clare, she had to step it up and go.

Key of C

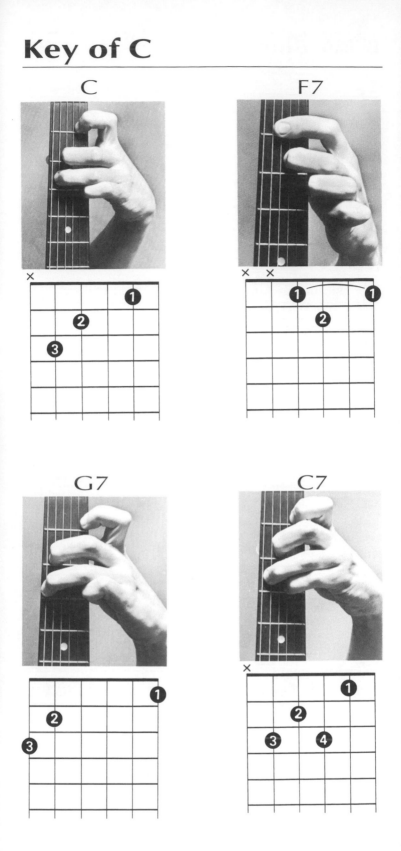

C

F7

G7

C7

Checkpoints

- Do not play the 5th or 6th strings with F7.

- This version of F7 is a bar chord. Make sure your index finger is straight and applying even pressure to all strings.

12-Bar Blues Progression in C

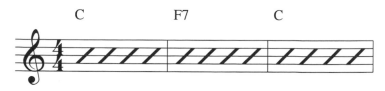

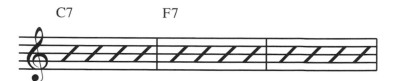

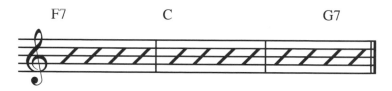

Right Hand: Blues Fingerpicking Pattern#1

Thumb picks a bass note.

Thumb, index and middle fingers pick the 3rd, 2nd, and 1st strings simultaneously.

Thumb picks a bass note.

Index finger picks the 2nd string.

Thumb picks the 3rd string.

Middle finger picks the 1st string.

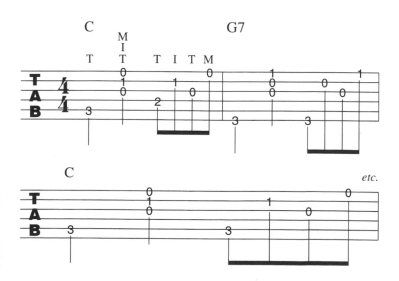

8-Bar Blues in C

Frankie and Johnny

Frankie and John - ny were lov-ers,____

Lord - y, how they____ could love.

Swore to be true__ to each oth-er,____ just as

true as the stars a - bove, He was her

man,_____ but he__ done her

wrong._____

Key of Em

Em

Am

B7

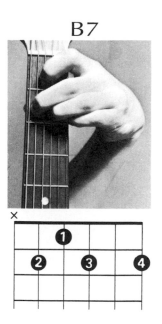

Checkpoints

- When playing B7, make sure your third finger is not muffling the 2nd string.

- Do not play the open 6th string with B7.

8-Bar Blues Progression in Em

①
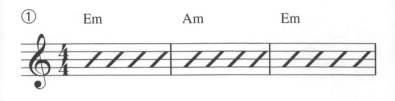

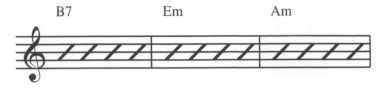

②
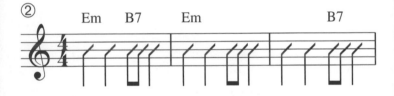

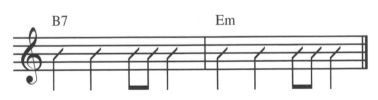

Right Hand: Blues Arpeggio #2

Thumb picks a bass note.

Index finger picks the 3rd string.

Middle finger picks the 2nd string.

Ring finger picks the 1st string.

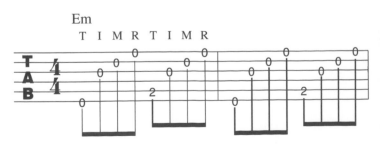

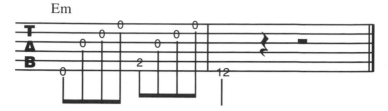

Darlin'

If I'd__ a known my cap-tain was blind,__

Dar-lin',_____ If I'd a known my

cap-tain was blind, Dar-lin',_____

If I'd__ a known my cap-tain was blind, I

would-n't have been to work un - til

half__ past nine,__ Dar-lin'._____

Key of Am

Am

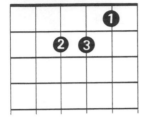

Dm

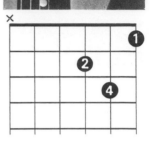

E7

Checkpoints

- Do not strum the 6th string with D7.

- Be sure that in the E7 chord your fourth finger stretches out to the 2nd string, third fret.

- When playing Dm, your third finger is lifted up out of the way of the strings.

8-Bar Blues Progressions in Am

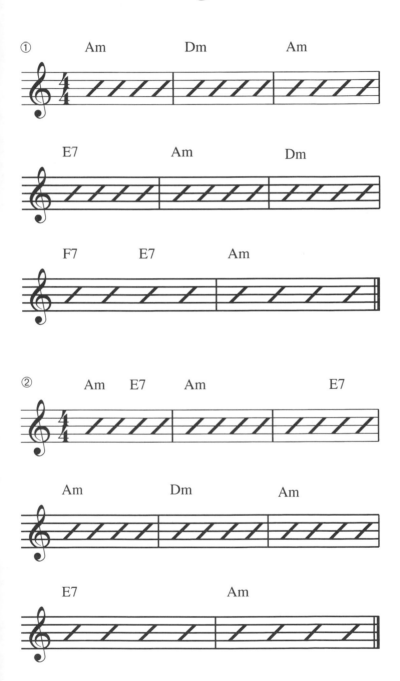

Right Hand: Blues Arpeggio #3

Thumb picks a bass note.

Index, middle, and ring fingers pick the 3rd, 2nd, and 1st strings simultaneously.

Thumb picks a bass note.

Index, middle, and ring fingers pick the 3rd, 2nd, and 1st strings separately.

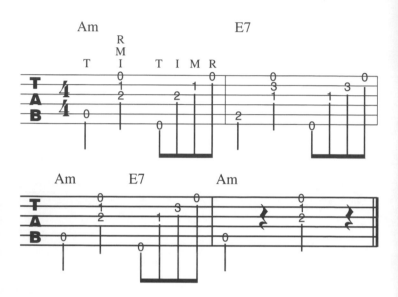

Saint James Infirmary

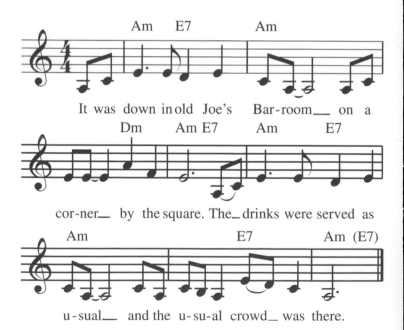

It was down in old Joe's   Bar-room___ on a

cor-ner___ by the square. The___drinks were served as

u-sual___ and the u-su-al crowd___ was there.

The Blues Form

As you have seen by now, most blues songs follow the same basic chord progression, usually a 12- or 8-bar pattern. Although there is some variation of chords within this structure, the basic form remains constant. Once you are thoroughly familiar with the blues form, you can play just about any blues song or instrumental, which is why the blues is a favorite progression when muslclans get together to Jam.

The most common blues form is the 12-bar progression, which utilizes the three most basic chords in any given key; the tonic (I), the subdominant (IV), and the dominant seventh (V7). Usually, the subdominant is played as a seventh chord with a more typical blues sound, so I have given them to you this way throughout the book.

Here are the basic chords in the five most widely used keys.

Key	Tonic (I)	Sub-dominant (IV7)	Dominant 7 (V7)
A	A	D7	E7
C	C	F7	G7
D	D	G7	A7
E	E	A7	B7
G	G	C7	D7

Other Blues Progressions

The following chord progressions are somewhat more complex than the standard 12- or 8-bar blues that we have been playing up to now. Practice these until they can be played without hesitation.

Key of C

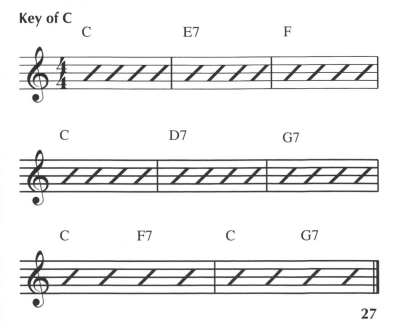

27

Key of G

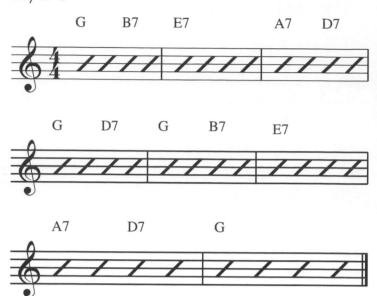

G   B7   E7   A7   D7

G   D7   G   B7   E7

A7   D7   G

Key of E

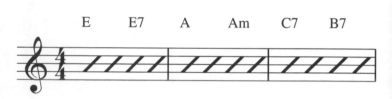
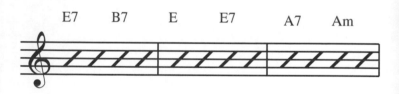

E   E7   A   Am   C7   B7

E7   B7   E   E7   A7   Am

B7   C7   B7   E

Key of A

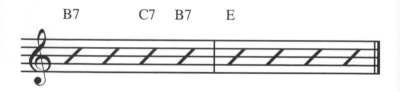

A   A7   D7

Dm   A   E7

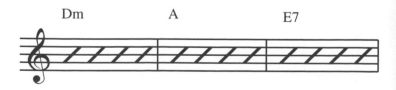

A   A7   D   Dm   A   F7   E7

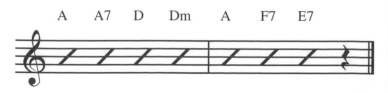

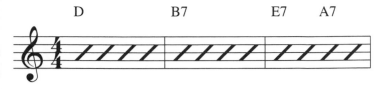

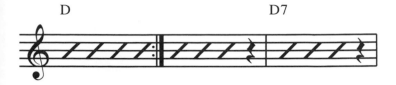

Stagolee

Well I was stand-in'_____ on the

cor-ner ___ when I heard my bull-dog ___

bark. He was bark -in' at the two men who were

gam - blin' in the ___ dark.

Bar Chords

These chords can be moved to any position on the fingerboard, enabling you to play blues in any key.

E Position

Major: F

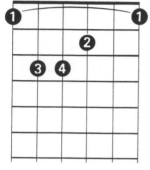

Seventh: F7

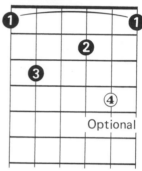

Optional

Minor: Fm

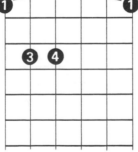

Checkpoints

- Keep your index finger straight, using your thumb to apply the necessary pressure to the strings. Pay special attention to the tone of the 1st, 2nd, and 6th strings.

- Each fret raises the chord by ½ step. Therefore, the E position with the bar on the second fret is F♯; on the third fret it is G, and so on.

Here is a chart of the chords in this position:

Fret	Major	Seventh	Minor
2nd	F#/G♭	F#7/G♭7	F#m/G♭m
3rd	G	G7	Gm
4th	G#/A♭	G#7/A♭7	G#m/A♭m
5th	A	A7	Am
6th	A#/B♭	A#/B♭7	A#m/B♭m
7th	B	B7	Bm
8th	C	C7	Cm

Right Hand: Strum with Moving Bass, Barred F Position

Thumb picks a bass note.

Index finger brushes up across the top two or three strings.

Try this with different positions on the fingerboard, using the barred F position.

Barred F Position

New Stranger Blues

31

A Position

Major:
A#/B♭

Seventh:
A#7/B♭7

Minor:
A#m/B♭m

Checkpoints

- Be sure your index finger is barring the strings accurately. Listen to the 1st, 5th, and 6th to see if they are fretting clearly.

- Be especially careful that you can hear the 3rd string when playing the seventh position.

- As in the E position chords, each fret raises the chord by ½ step.

Here is a chart of the chords in this position:

Fret	Major	Seventh	Minor
2nd	B	B7	Bm
3rd	C	C7	Cm
4th	C♯/D♭	C♯7/D♭7	C♯m/D♭m
5th	D	D7	Dm
6th	D♯/E♭	D♯7/E♭7	D♯m/E♭m
7th	E	E7	Em
8th	F	F7	Fm

Right Hand: Strum with Moving Bass, Barred A Position

Thumb picks a bass note.

Index finger brushes up across the top two or three strings.

Barred A

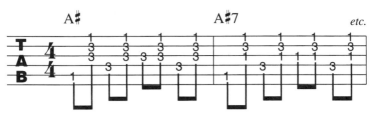

12-Bar Blues in A♭

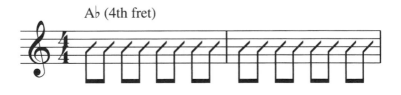

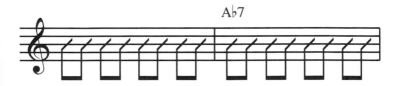

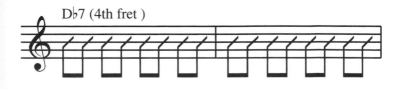

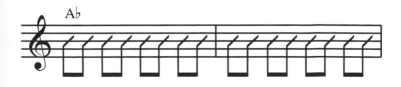

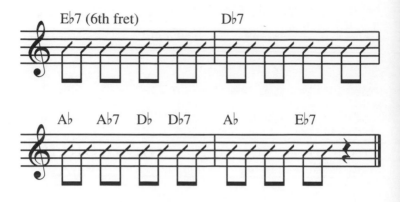

Sportin' Life Blues

I got a let-ter__ from my home. Most of my friends are__ dead and gone. That old night life,__ that old sport-in' life is kill-in' me.__

Movable Seventh Chords

In these positions it will be necessary to damp the open strings (prevent them from sounding) by touching them lightly with the left hand while fretting the notes you need.

Position 1: movable C

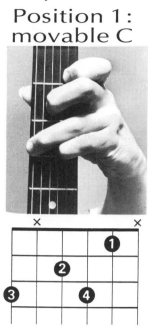

Position 2: movable B7

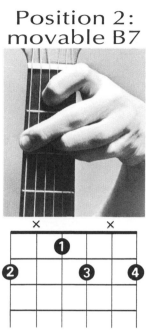

Position 3: movable F7

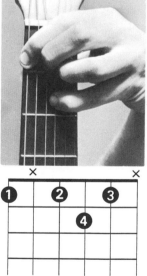

Checkpoints

- In the C7 position, damp the 5th string with your third finger, and the 1st string with your first finger.

- In the B7 position, damp the 5th string with your second finger, and the 2nd string with your third finger.

- In the F7 position, the 5th string is damped by your first finger, and the 1st string by your third finger.

- As with the bar chords, each fret represents ½ step. Therefore, moving the C7 position up the neck would give you C♯7/D♭7, D7, D♯7/E♭7, and so on.

Blues Progression with Seventh Chords

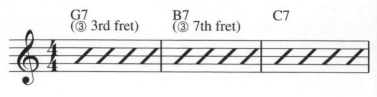

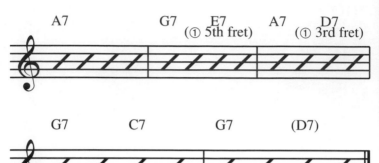

Right Hand : Blues Strum #3

Index finger brushes up across the high strings.

Index (and middle) finger brushes down.

Index finger brushes up.

Index (and middle) finger brushes down, followed by a quick damping of the strings with the open hand.

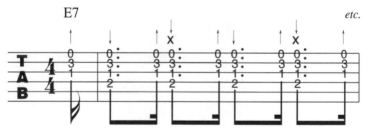

The 2:19 Train

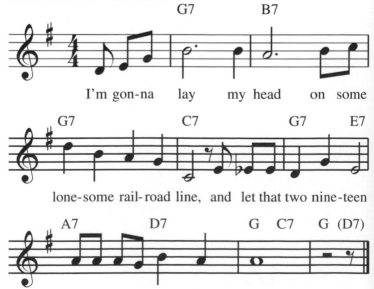

I'm gon-na lay my head on some lone-some rail-road line, and let that two nine-teen pa-ci-fy my wor-ried mind.

Diminished Chords

The diminished chords are indicated by °7 after the chord letter. They are named after any note of the chord.

A°7, C°7,
D♯°7/E♭°7,
F♯°7/G♭°7

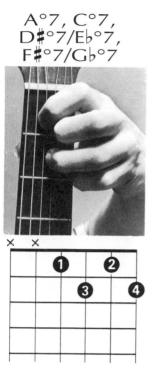

A♯°7/B♭°7,
C♯°7/D♭°7,
E°7, G°7,

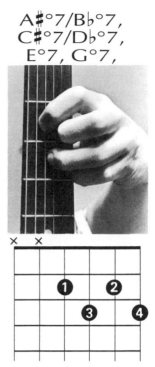

B°7, D°7, F°7,
G♯°7/A♭°7

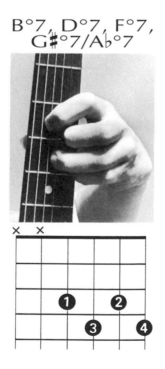

Checkpoints

- You can move these diminished chords up the neck as long as you do not play the 5th or 6th strings.

- The chords repeat in a new inversion every three frets.

Practice Progressions

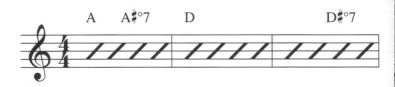

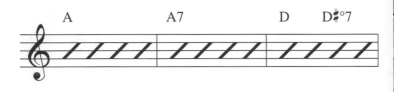

Right Hand: Blues Fingerpicking Pattern #2

Thumb picks a bass note and the middle finger picks the 1st string at the same time.

Index finger picks the 2nd string.

Thumb picks the 3rd string.

Middle finger picks the 1st string.

Thumb picks a bass note.

Index finger picks the 2nd string.

Thumb picks the 3rd string.

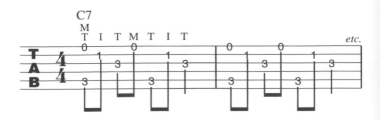

Make Me a Pallet on Your Floor

Make me a pal - let on your floor; —

_____ make me a pal - let on your

floor. _____ Make it soft, make it

low, so my good gal won't know.

Make me a pal - let on your floor. _____

Movable Chords on the High Strings

These chord positions can be used very effectively for playing melodic breaks or harmonies while singing or accompanying other instruments. It is only necessary to avoid or damp the bass strings when they do not fit in the chord you are playing.

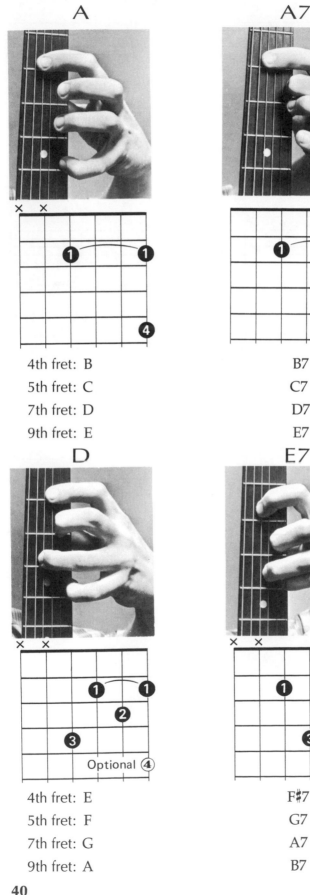

A	A7
4th fret: B	B7
5th fret: C	C7
7th fret: D	D7
9th fret: E	E7

D	E7
4th fret: E	F♯7
5th fret: F	G7
7th fret: G	A7
9th fret: A	B7

40

Practice Progression

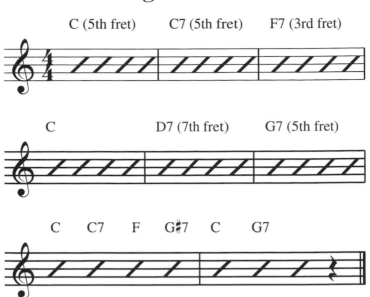

| C (5th fret) | C7 (5th fret) | F7 (3rd fret) |

| C | D7 (7th fret) | G7 (5th fret) |

| C | C7 | F | G#7 | C | G7 |

Right Hand: Variations on Fingerpicking Pattern #2

Use the A and A7 movable chords on page 28.

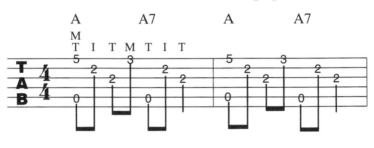

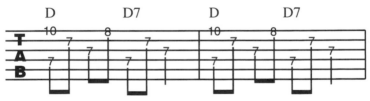

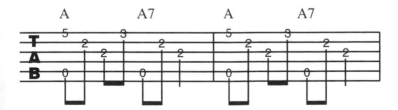

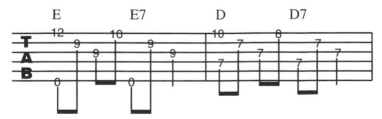

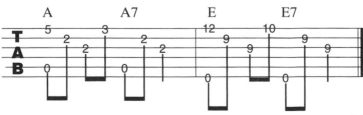

Betty and Dupree

Bet-ty told Du-pree,— I want a dia-mond

ring.— Yes, Bet-ty told Du-pree,—

I want a dia-mond ring.—

— Du-pree said to Bet-ty, I'll

get you most a-ny — thing.

Some Extra Hints for Playing the Blues

The Turnaround

You have probably noticed that most blues stanzas end with a chord progression that leads your ear back to the beginning of the next verse. This is called the turnaround, and can be played either with chords or melodically. Here are some typical chord turnarounds:

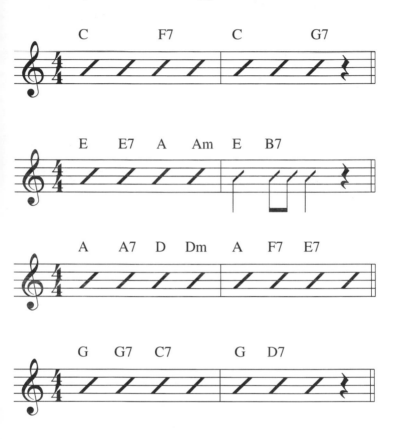

Read the following tablature carefully to play different kinds of turnarounds.

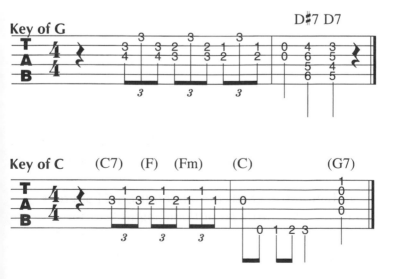

Key of E

Key of A

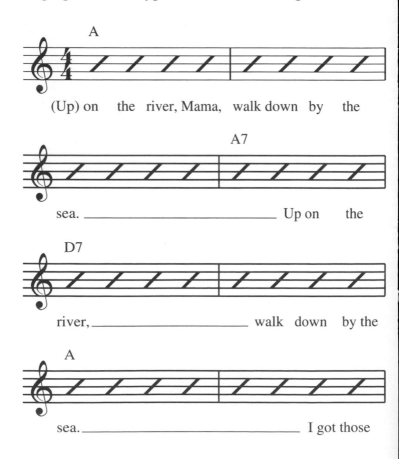

Fills

Most 12-bar blues songs consist of three lines of singing: the first line is sung, then repeated, followed by a third line which rhymes with the other two. Each line has approximately the same number of beats. Take a look at *Matchbox Blues* (page 11) and see how the singing fits into a typical 12-bar blues song.

A

(Up) on   the   river, Mama,   walk down   by   the

A7

sea. _____ Up on   the

D7

river,_____ walk   down   by the

A

sea._____ I got those

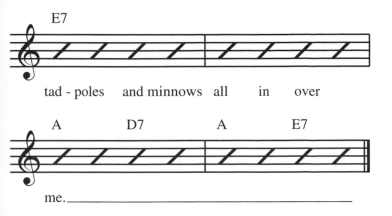

E7

tad - poles   and minnows   all   in   over

A   D7   A   E7

me._____

Notice that there are "holes" in the singing where the guitar usually provides an "answer" in the form of a blues fill or riff. Here are some typical fills that you can practice in different keys. With slight variation, these fills can be used as turnarounds.

Key of A

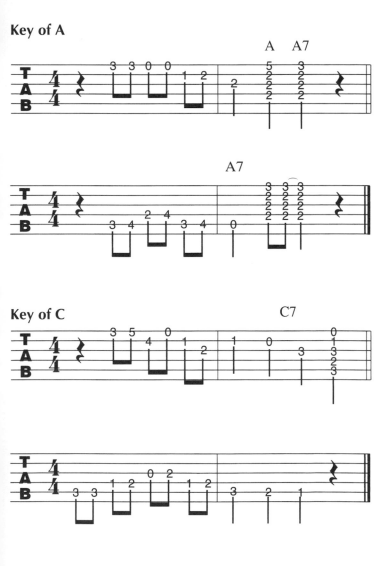

Key of C

Key of G

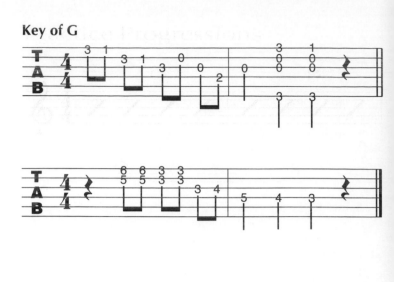

Key of E

E7

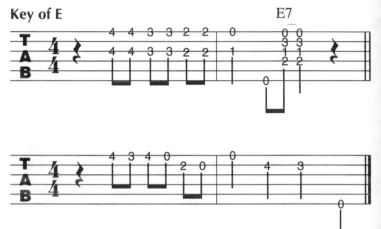